Acting Fundamentals Level 2

Teacher Edition

By

Tracy Brooke

Acting Fundamentals Level 2

Objective: Students will increase in awareness and skill set applying fundamental principles to a performance.

Lesson 1 Relaxation	Lesson 2 Exploring Scripts	Lesson 3 Concentration	Lesson 4 Know your scene	Lesson 5 Imagination
Lesson 6 Scene Setting	Lesson 7 Using imagination	Lesson 8 Listening	Lesson 9 Objectives	Lesson 10 Emotions
Lesson 11 Tactics	Lesson 12 Characterization (15 Leys to characterization will be done soon)	Lesson 13 Performances	Lesson 13 Continued	Lesson 13 Continued
Library Days	Library Days	Game Day	Game Day	Game Day

Contents

Title	Page
Lesson 1 Relaxation	4
Lesson 2 Exploring a script	6
Lesson 3 Concentration	10
Lesson 4 Know your scene	14
Lesson 5 Imagination	16
Lesson 6 Scene Setting	20
Lesson 7 using Imagination	23
Lesson 8 Listening	27
Lesson 9 Objective	29
Lesson 10 Emotions	33
Lesson 11 Tactics	36
Lesson 12 Characterization	39
Lesson 13 Performance	41
Library Days	42
Game Days	43
Evaluation	44
Quiz	46
Scene Scoring Worksheet	52
Participation Points	53
Class Management	56

Performance Fundamentals Level 2
Lesson 1: Relaxation

Objective: Students will demonstrate physical and mental alertness by improvising greetings.

Section 1: Intellectual

Relaxation Worksheet and Review

Section 2: Game Play

Game 1: Students will sit comfortably on the floor with back straight but not stiff. They will close their eyes and just feel their body as they breathe.
    a. Have the students focus on the out breath letting all of the air out of the lungs and body in order to find the moment of "rest."
    b. picture the energy of the breath flowing into the entire body.
    c. Focus on the breath in the lower ribs.
    d. Focus on the movement of the mid back.
    e. Focus on the whole body breathing having every part participate in the flow of air.
    f. Have the students stand up and sense the change in balance of the body and change of tension. Help the students recognize the restful, alert state.

Game 2: Physical Relaxation. Have the students participate in stretching and relaxing exercises. Have them bend over at the waist and touch the floor in the middle, to the left leg, and then the right leg. Then come up vertebra by vertebra. Have the student's stretch out each of the major body muscles.

Game 3: Mental Relaxation: Imagine that you are a balloon slowly filling with air as you breathe in. Take in more air, and more and more until you fill the classroom .Now picture yourself filling up the entire city. Now keep stretching up, growing bigger and bigger. You find yourself floating up above the school. Visualize the school as you float above it. You float up above the city. Picture the city as you look down upon it. You float up and up and picture the landscape of the country and the world. You keep floating up until you reach the moon. Picture the stars. Smell the cold air and feel the rough texture of the moon. Now you begin to shrink. Slowly you come back to the earth. Picture the feeling and sight of the earth coming in to view. You shrink and see the country becoming even smaller and come back above the city. You shrink until you see the school and you are back in the room. Smell the room and visualize the walls and floors. Feel the texture of your pants on your skin. And now open your eyes. Wiggle your fingers and toes. Count all of the object in the room that are red.

Game 4: Visualize yourself walking into a room. What can you smell? Is the room old or new? You notice a desk in the corner. Is it a small or large desk? Is the wood bright and polished or old and warn? You notice a letter poking out of a drawer. What sort of paper is it? Is it lined or stationary? Is it fresh or has it been there for a while. Take the letter out of the drawer. Open it up and read it. Wait a minute. You fold the letter up and place it back in the drawer. Notice the resistance of the drawer as you close it. You look around the room and walk out. Listen to your foot steps as you walk out of the room. Picture yourself walking up to the school and into this room. Now open your eyes and look around.
        Have each student say what was written on the letter they "read".

Section 3 Scene Work:

Step 1: Pick a scene and a partner
Step 2: Tell the instructor who your partner is and what scene you will use for points.

Section 4
Assessment:
Each student things of their characters in the scene and chooses the dominant character trait and point of view of the world. Each scene group will work together. The partners will stand at opposite ends of the playing space. When they reach the center, the students greet each other without using words in character. Have the students then answer questions from the instructor concerning the character and greeting.

Materials:
Scenes

Relaxation

Knowing how to control your muscles by relaxing, and tensing gives you the opportunity to create a wide variety of physicalizations on the stage. As a performer, you need to be able to let go of any stressors in your day, to relax and release your personal stressors and go to a neutral place so you can present a character on the stage.

After a performance, you need to be able to relax, let go of any stressors of the play or the character and go back to your life fully capable of being yourself and living your life.

The body is the actors tool and taking care of your body supports your performance skills.

1. Why should a performer know who to relax?
Gives control over the body, the actors tool.

Give it a try:

Daily De-stressors
Pop a prune (great brain food to combat stress)
Visualize a vacation
Say: This to Shall Pass
Count to sixty and pause before responding
Take a moment and focus on your breathe making sure it is deep and rhythmic

Long Term De-Stressors
Free Style Journal Write ten minutes a day
Exercise
Sleep regular hours, and long enough.

Performance Fundamentals Level 2

Lesson 2: Exploring The Script

Objective: Students will understand the importance of script analysis by verbally explaining their scene to the teacher.

Section 1: Intellectual

Worksheet and review. Refer to scene scoring worksheet for students to write their beat of action analysis work in as this unit progresses.

Section 2: Games

Game 1. Relaxation: Close your eyes and think about your left arm. Say three times, my left arm is relaxed. Go through each part of your body consciously choosing to relax.

Game 2: Every one stands in a circle. One person goes into the hall for a second. Choose a leader. They are going to start a movement and everyone else is going to follow. After a moment or two they will change the movement and everyone will follow along. The person is called in from the hall. When they get to the center of the circle, the leader begins the movement. The person in the center tries to figure out who is starting the movements.

Game 3. Zing / Zong: Have the class stand in a circle one person says zing looking to the left. The person next to them then looks to the person at the left saying zing. If a student looks to the right, the word and direction changes. The student looks to the right and says zong, so the next student looks to the right and says zong. Get the word direction going quickly.

Game 4. Improvisation: One student is interviewing for a job to buy something important to them. The interviewer needs to have a clear job that he is looking to hire someone for. (See Theatre Machine II pg 2)

Section 3: Scene Work

Allow your students to choose their scene partners and to choose a script. Have them show you the script to record the information. In their workbook, they have the following assignments to do during scene work time.

Scene Work

With your scene partner do the following work and check it off when you are done.

- o   Read through the script three times
- o   High light your lines
- o   # what you and others say about you

Section 4 Assessment:

Students will show their scenes to the teacher and say what their scene is about for participation points.

Script Exploration

The script is the performers road map to success.

Prepare yourself for script exploration by reading a script three times like a novel. Read for fun, be curious, ask questions but do not make any judgment calls or hurry into an analysis work. You are creating a foundation for the script analysis by reading just for fun.

1. How should you prepare to do script analysis?
Read the script three times like a novel.

The first part of script exploration is to understand the structure and the flow of the play. Mark in your script where the inciting incident is, where are the major events or happenings of the play. Mark where the climax or highest point of action is, and notice the falling action or the tying up of all loose ends. When you know the flow of the play, your job as the actor is to supply the energy to lead the audience on the journey through the action up to the climax. When everyone in a production team knows the flow of the play, then the group synergy leads the play on its natural rhythm and supplies the energy necessary to build the play.

2. What is the first part of script analysis?
Understand the structure and flow of the play.

The next part of script exploration is more personal to your character. Highlight your lines. Underline any stage description or character comment that gives you clues to your character. Then look at the scenes you are in and circle the lines of your scene partners that trigger you to speak and respond to them. Mark your entrances and exits and pay attention to how your character builds the show.

3. What is the second thing to do for script analysis?
Highlighting entrances, exits, lines, and look for clues to reveal your character.

The third part of script analysis is detail oriented. Draw a line after each beat of action. Each beat of action will be one bit of action. When the dialogue changes, when people enter or exit, or when the desires change – so does your beat of action. Draw a line after each beat. Number your beats of action and on another page, write the number, then write what your want is in the next column. The third column is where you write your tactics. The fourth column is where you write your obstacles.

4. What is the third thing to do with script analysis?
Know your beats of action.

The fourth part of script analysis is day dreaming. Create your character sketch, create your relationships, imagine your moment before, create your exits and where you are going. Day dream and imagine a full and rich life for your character drawing on your life experiences and observations from other peoples lives.

5. What is the fourth part of script analysis?
Daydreaming

Once you have done all your script analysis and preparation, you let it go. You trust that your work is there and step into the world of the play as if it was real… as if it was you.

6. What do you do after all the script analysis is done?
Let it go and trust that it has created your creative foundation.

Performance Fundamentals Level 2

Lesson 3: Concentration and observation

Objective: Students will demonstrate their ability to feel physically and emotionally by performing a group pantomime.

Section 1 Intellectual Time:

Concentration Worksheet and review
.

Section 2

Points: Break the class into teams. If the students win the different games they receive a point. If they misbehave a point is taken away. The team with the most points wins.

Game 1: The students will stand in lines. The person at one end whispers a sentence to the person next in line. This person in turn passes it to the next person and so on until everyone in line has heard the sentence. Then the last person repeats the sentence out loud. Which ever team says the right sentence, wins.

Game 2: The students will be instructed to partner up with someone on their team. One partner is given a fortune cookie. They open it and read the fortune. The other partner will give a response of over three words. The exchange goes on until each person has responded at least five times. If each accurately and effectively do five responses a point is earned for their team.

Game 3: What are you doing game. Two students stand in front of the class. One starts pantomiming an action. The other student says "what are you doing?" The first student keeps pantomiming the action but says a different action. The second student must start pantomiming the action. The first student then asks, "What are you doing? " The second student keeps their pantomime going and says a completely different action, the first student must start pantomiming this new action and so on. After ten effective pantomimes a point is earned.

Game 4: Each of the students will think of an animal and how it moves. A student is chosen to go first. He or she will go to the front and begin circling around the playing area as that animal. When others are certain they know of the animal the student is playing, they will go up and join him or her. When the "herd" is the entire team, the group winds a point.

Section 3 Scene Work

Explain to the students the following assignment:
This is located in their unit work book.

Check off The List while You Work With Your Scene Partner:

- ☐ Read the Script. On The back of the script, write the events of the scene. What are the major things that happen in this script? Discuss the major events of the scene with your scene partner.

- ☐ With Your scene Partner, Read the Script.

- ☐ Perform The Scene Without The Script to the best of your ability focusing on the major happenings.

- ☐ Perform The Scene With The Script.

Section 4 Assessment:

The teacher will divide the class into their teams. The group will figure out what they are going to be as they cross the playing area. They all have to be part of the same thing, a train, a caterpillar. They need to hold on to each other in an appropriate way and do their best to convey to the rest of the class what they are. It must be cone complete crossing of the area. If the team does if well, they receive a point.

Materials:
Fortune Cookies

Concentration

The actor has a dual role.

As the actor you must concentrate on lines, staging, other characters, props, costumes, movements, and audience response. Practice these skills so that they become second nature. Imagine your scenes so that your mind knows the moves and feel of the character and when you are on stage you can have the actors role be secondary in your mind.

1. What must the actor concentrate on?
Lines staging, props, movements

As the character concentrate on the characters needs and the desire to get them met. IF you make the characters life interesting enough, you will concentrate on the goal and truly listen and respond in character.

2. What must the character concentrate on?
The objectives and getting them met.

Imagining "the fourth wall" helps with concentration. Pretend that there is a wall between you and the audience and let the audience slip into the back of your mind. If you are performing a monologue look right above the audiences heads so that you can keep the illusion of the fourth wall in your mind.

3. What is the fourth wall?
Pretending that there is a screen or wall between you and the audience....

Observation

Watch people carefully and take notes on who people are and how they respond to the environment, to others, and in coversations. Do not judge people or make criticisms of how people live and respond. Your job as a performer is to observe and remember a variety of people and honest life responses so that you can create believable characters.

4. Why should you spend time observing people and places?
Creates truthful knowledge to how people behave and respond for accurate presentations.

Take time to sit in restaurants and watch the people interact with each other. Watch different age groups and pay attention to how they walk, talk, and interact with each other. Notice clothing, hair, looks, gestures, mannerisms, dialogue and any thing else that catches your attention free of any judgment or criticism.

Performance Fundamentals Level 2
Lesson 4: Knowing Your Scene

Objective: Students will understand the importance of script analysis by improvising the main idea of their script in front of a class.

Section 1: Intellectual

Worksheet and review

Section 2: Games

Game 1: Mental Relaxation: Imagine that you are a balloon slowly filling with air as you breathe in. Take in more air, and more and more until you fill the classroom .Now picture yourself filling up the entire city. Now keep stretching up, growing bigger and bigger. You find yourself floating up above the school. Visualize the school as you float above it. You float up above the city. Picture the city as you look down upon it. You float up and up and picture the landscape of the country and the world. You keep floating up until you reach the moon. Picture the stars. Smell the cold air and feel the rough texture of the moon. Now you begin to shrink. Slowly you come back to the earth. Picture the feeling and sight of the earth coming in to view. You shrink and see the country becoming even smaller and come back above the city. You shrink until you see the school and you are back in the room. Smell the room and visualize the walls and floors. Feel the texture of your pants on your skin. And now open your eyes. Wiggle your fingers and toes. Count all of the object in the room that are red.

Game 2: Simple Action. Give a student a simple action like washing the dishes or brushing their teeth. They perform the action and the class tries to guess what it is.

Game 3: Two students cross the room and meet in the middle. One person is a banker, the other person is a lottery winner. Another group one can be an old lady and another person is a thug. Give a definite situation for the greeting in the middle of the room.

Game 4: Interview Improvs: One person has a specific job and is an interviewer. Another student has a definite need and has to get the job.

Section 3: Student Work

Each student has a copy of what is expected in group time in their unit work book.

Scene Work

With your scene partner do the following work and check it off when you are done.

- o   Read through the script and ....
- o   Mark where the inciting moment is
- o   Mark where the climax of the scene is
- o   Draw a light bulb where revelations and discoveries are
- o   @ at turning points or changes in action
- o   Create a set

Section 4: Assessment

Students will improvise a one minute synopsis of their script.

Knowing Your Scene

Read through the play and decide on a theme. What is the story trying to say? What is the message of the play that everyone in the production can come together and use all of the elements of the play to tell the story and reveal the theme. Knowing the theme unifies the cast and crew into one purpose and one direction for the story telling process.

1. Why do you need to know the theme?
Theme is the purpose that unifies a cast and crew.

What are the events in the play? What happens? Know the conflict in every scene, in every character, and know all of the action from the beginning all the way through to the end of the play. Know the events, know how your character plays into the events. If you do not know the events then you have not rooted your character or truly invested in the world of the play. Knowing the events gives you strong motivation and purpose for your presence on stage.

2. Why should you know the events of the play?
To know what your purpose is, to know what you are doing.

Know where the scene takes place and how this environment shapes your play, your character and your responses. You have to know where you are and how you feel about this to give purpose and reason to your character and to your lines.

The actor needs to know where the discoveries are. What information is given to your character that is new to them? Create memories and expectations for the character so that when this information is given to you, you respond honestly with new information that will shape your characters objectives and tactics.

The actor needs to know where the turning points are. Purposefully create a situation where the character expects different information and is surprised by the new information. The actor needs to know if they won or lost, respond appropriately and adjust in a new direction to get his or her needs met.

The actor also needs to know where the climax is and expend the right amount of energy through the play to lead up to this highest moment in the play.

Your character may be defeated in the end – the character does not know that. Play every moment of the scene as if it was real . . . as if it was happening for the first time . . . and do everything you can to win your goal fully expecting to win.

3. What are three things the actor needs to know when exploring the events of a play?
Where he or she is, what are the discoveries, where are the turning points.

Performance Fundamentals Level 2

Lesson 5: Imagination

Objective: The students will demonstrate their ability to freely connect emotions with actions by pantomiming characters.

Section 1 Intellectual Work:

Imagination Worksheet and review

Section 2 Game play

Game 1: Have each student decide what animal they would choose to become if they could not be a human being. Have them spend a few moments thinking about the animal and how it moves and walks and carries itself. Then have the students stand and begin to walk around becoming the animal.

Game 2: Play music and have each of the students draw with colors on paper or put abstract stage makeup on their faces according to the mood evoked from the music. Pass the picture to a different student who writes a sentence about the picture. Place the pictures on the floor or wall, and pass the sentences to a third student. Have the students try to figure which sentence goes to which paper.

Game 3: Have the student's perform fairy tales in gibberish.
Gibberish is nonsense sounds that you use to convey an idea. Get rid of the words we use and focus on conveying the sense of the word in this improvisational game.

Section 3 Scene Work

Explain to the students the following assignment:
This is located in their unit work book.

Scene Work

Check off the boxes when you and your scene partners have completed the work.

- o ☐ Read the scene. Use the "Bounding Ball Improv" You can only speak when holding a ball. Throw the ball to your scene partner during or after your line. This helps the actor learn to connect to their scene partner.

- o ☐ Read the scene and use the "contact" Improvisation. You must make physical contact in an appropriate way with the actor you are speaking to before each new speech, or sentence. This helps the actor learn to connect to their scene partner.

- o ☐ Read the scene and use the "packing pistols" improve. Pretend to fire guns while you speak. This improve helps the actor know who they are speaking to and convey what you want.

- o ☐ Read the scene and then do the "tennis" rehearsal. Swat pretend tennis balls as you speak. This improv helps the actors pick up the pace and achieve a normal pacing for conversations.

Section 4

Assessment: Have one student arrange another student in a certain stance or posture. The student who was arranged will then begin an improvisation with the person who arranged them.

Materials:
Music, paper, crayons, balls

Imagination

Use all five senses when you imagine. Imagine what some one smells like. What their voice sounds like. Imagine what their touch felt like and how your physical body felt around them. What did you see? What colors does the person remind you of. Use all five senses to recreate memories that are full and rich and vibrant. When you use all of your senses to recreate a memory for yourself or your character, you will create a rich inner life that will make your performances come alive.

1. Why do you use all five senses when you imagine?
To make memories real and strong.

Use your imagine to create a character. Imagine five life events that shape this person and creates who they are today. Draw on your own life experiences and the experiences of family and friends to create five deep and moving life experiences.

Use your imagination to create the moment before you enter the scene. Who are you and what are you doing? Why do you go into this scene and what do you want when you are in it? When you exit – where do you go and why? When you say you are leaving, make sure you are fully committed to leaving and use your imagination to create a rich and full exit scene.

Use your imagination to create relationships on the stage. Who are you talking to. What other experiences have you had with this person. How do you feel in this space and with this person. Create a life relationship with this person using all five senses so when you respond to the other person on stage the history is there giving a believable scene.

Use your imagination to create "triggers" for your lines. What do the other characters say to you? Where in their dialogue does a memory or a thought get triggered that propels you to speak?

Imagine what this person wants in their life, in this play, in this scene and in this moment and then use all of your focus, energy, imagination, and self to create this person and do everything possible to meet these wants.

It all starts with a little bit of imagination.

2. What are three things a performer uses their imagination to create?
Character, moment before, relationships, triggers, life objectives

Performance Fundamentals Level 2

Lesson 6: Scene Setting

Objective: Students will demonstrate the importance of setting in their script by improvising their scene in a setting opposite of what their scene calls for.

Section 1: Intellectual

Worksheet and review

Section 2: Games

Game 1: Each of the students will think of an animal and how it moves. A student is chosen to go first. He or she will go to the front and begin circling around the playing area as that animal. When others are certain they know of the animal the student is playing, they will go up and join him or her. When the "herd" is the entire team, the group winds a point.

Game 2: Students will pantomime a walk through. Walking through jello, walking through a desert, walking through a forest, etc…

Game 3: Patterns. The students arrange themselves on the stage floor in any pattern open to the audience. When everyone is up on stage they freeze. Then rearrange into another pattern. Pattern can be at a restaurant, bus stop, dance hall, work location….

Game 4: Each student will pantomime a location and students will guess where they are located such as a hospital, a school, a church, a dance….

Game 5: Machine. One student starts with a sound and a movement. Students come and connect to the first student with a different sound and movement creating a machine. When everyone is up have the machine go faster and louder and then break going smaller and quieter.

Section 3: Scene Work

Each student has a copy of scene work expectations in their book

Scene Work

With your scene partner do the following work and check it off when you are done.

- o Discuss the setting and how you feel in this space

- o Work on making your set more real

- o Write your blocking in the script. Make sure each person has three moves.

- o Rehearse your scene focusing on the setting and movements and how you feel in this space.

Section 4: Assessment

Students will improvise their scene in a very different location then what the playwright intended. Other students may join the improvisation as waiters etc....

Scene Setting

The physical location of the scene will affect your characterization.
What time of day is it?
What mood are you in?
What tone of voice do you use in this setting? You will talk different in a restaurant then you will a living room of a friend.
What is the temperature? Are you dressed appropriately?
What season of the year is it.

Know the physical aspects of the setting.

Then start exploring the emotional qualities of the set.
How do you feel in this place.
What are three or four events that have happened to you in this place before? When you enter the set, that rich life of events will be there affecting your presentation and increase your believability.

Think about the people you interact with in the scene. How do you feel about them and how do you respond to them. Who are they in this setting and how does it affect them and their behavior to you.

The third part of scene setting is staging it effectively for the audience. Know the purpose of the scene. Who is the dominant character. Place them in dominant stage positions where they can have the audience focus. Do you want your audience to wonder who will win an argument or if the girl will fall in love, place the scene down stage center. When you want a finality to the scene and a firm decision made, place the action in down left stage. If you want someone to look powerful, place them at a higher level than another character. IF you want the audience to not trust someone, have them enter and cross from the right to the left rather than the way our eyes have been t rained to flow from left to right. Knowing some simple staging techniques can add power to your scene.

1. Why should you know the physical location of the scene?
It affects a persons behavior and thoughts.

2. Why should you know the emotional qualities of the set?
It affects a persons behavior and thoughts.

3. Why should you know the relationships with the people within this location
It affects a persons behavior and thoughts.

4. What does the actor/director need to know about set and staging?
Who is the dominant character and what emotion you want to evoke in the audience.

Performance Fundamentals Level 2
Lesson 7: Using The Imagination

Objective: The students will show their ability to think creatively with improvisation.

Section 1 Intellectual Time:

Character Sketch

Section 2:

Game 1: The Students will receive an individual improvisational scenario. They will take the time to perform the scenario in front of the class.

Game 2: Freeze. One person sits on a bench. A second student approaches the bench and strikes up a conversation as a crazy person who thinks he or she is someone else. A student might be an alien, a priest, or a ballerina. Students can freeze in at any time, take the place of the crazy person and become anyone....

Game 3: Group improvisation. Students will get into a group of four to five people. They will come up with a location and a situation to perform in front of the class. The class will guess where they are.

Section 3 Scene Work

Scene Work

- **Step 1:** read the scene and then improve it in gibberish. This helps develop the meaning and messages of the scene.

- **Step 2:** Read the scene and then improve it while dancing. This helps to find the movement of the character based on wants and needs in the scene.

- **Step 3:** Read the scene and then improve it while laughing, crying, or chuckling through it. This improve supports the actor in finding different emotional levels of the scene.

- **Step 4:** read the scene and improve it is slow motion. This improvisation helps you find the moments of pause and deliberateness of the scene.

Section 4

Assessment:

The students will perform the moment before their scenes begin in front of the class.

Materials:

Improv starters for game 1.

Using The Imagination

You have imagined your character, you have imagined your given circumstances which are the life events and environment that shapes your character, you have done fun and wild improvisations. Now is the time to use your imagination for the greater good of your performance.

The actor needs to build a bridge between the intellectual side of script analysis and the creative aspect of performances.

Awareness is the first key to bridge building.

In your script you have marked how the play structure goes and you are aware of how to build the energy to match the playwrights intention.

You have marked revelations, turning points, and circled other peoples lines that trigger memories that cause you to say your lines.

Next you created memories and a life full of experiences for your character including how they feel in the setting and with the other people in the play. The awareness factor comes in by creating images that represent your life experiences. Look through your script and draw the images that come to mind with the lines or events of the play. When that scene comes, your preparation work will be there and you will remember the experiences of the character and they will motivate the lines and subtext of your performance.

After you worked hard on script analysis, you began to play lots of improvisations exploring different options, different rhythms, and the flow of your scene or play. When a certain flow of an improv worked well for you, be aware. Know that the playing tennis improv really helped with the pace of dialogue. Draw a tennis racket in the margin of your script so when you get to that point, your creativity will be reminded to pick up the pace in that scene.

The second key to using your imagination is trust. You have to trust yourself that the prep work will springboard your creativity. You have to trust the other performers to be equally engaged. You have to trust your audience will suspend disbelief and invest in the world you have created.

Trust is gained through kindness. Be nice to yourself, be nice to others. As you build people up with kindness and service, the creative possibilities quantify and magnify.

1. What are the two keys to using your imagination as specified in this unit?
Awareness and trust.

Character sketch

Draw a picture in each block representing the life you have explored for this character.

Life event:	Life event:
Life event:	Life event:

Setting

Situation that's happened here before:	Situation that's happened here before:
Situation that's happened here before:	Situation that's happened here before:

Relationships

Experience with this person:	Experience with this person:
Experience with this person:	Experience with this person:

Performance Fundamentals Level 2

Lesson 8: Listening

Objective: The students will demonstrate active listening by improvising their characters thoughts between dialogue.

Section 1 Intellectual Time:

Listening Worksheet and review

Section 2

Game 1: Word association game. One persona says a word, the next says something that the previous word reminds them of and so on.

Game 2: Have the students perform their scenes playing the listening game. Before they give their line, they must restate what their partner just said.

Section 3 Scene Work

Scene Work

- o ☐ Check off the boxes when you and your scene partner do the scene work:

- o ☐ Have a third person watch the script while you perform it for line memorization check.

- o ☐ Read the scene then improve it "soul" style. Using old gospel style "soul" do your scene! This helps you to find excitement and joy in your script.

- o ☐ Read the scene and then improve it singing. This helps you find energy and different levels and rhythms in your script.

- o ☐ Have a third person watch the scene reading the script while you perform it for a line memorization check.

Section 4

Assessment: The students will improve their scenes speaking their secret thoughts about everything, paying special not to what their scene partners are saying to them.

Listening

Listening is an active skill. When someone is speaking the other person is thinking, planning, and remembering things. Listening is reacting to thoughts and words.

Listening has sub text. Know what you are thinking – what you want the other person to see – and what you are hiding form the other person.

Listening is not a cue. Know what triggers your line well before the last word is spoken by the other person. Its o.k. to interrupt, overlap, or cut someone off. It happens in real life.

Know the inner life of your character and their listening and speaking style. Does their mind race and their words come out fast, do they think and carefully respond. Find a music instrument that reminds you of the character and experiment with listening and responding as if you were that instrument.

Improv's to help with listening:
Shadow rehearsal. Have a student follow you around stage asking you questions about what you think and feel concerning the other characters, events and dialogues.

Packing Pistols. Every one pretends to have guns. You fire your gun and move around the stage during your lines. This helps you to learn who to deliver your line to and in what manner.

Playing Tennis. This is where you and your scene partner pretend to have tennis rackets and hit a pretend ball back and forth. This helps with line deliver, reception, and rebuttal. How you hit the ball and respond to the ball shows a lot about the subtext of the character.

Subtext: Change all the dialogue to be "on the nose" dialouge. Say exactly what is on your characters mind. Try the scene again with the dialogue and see if the subtext is stronger when you listen and respond to each other.

1. _T_ T/F listening is an active Skill.

2. _F_ T/F listening is waiting for a cue

Performance Fundamentals Level 2
Lesson 9: Know your objective

Student Objective: Students will demonstrate the need to show an audience what they are doing by pantomime their scene in front of the class.

Section 1: Intellectual

Worksheet and review. Refer to the scene scoring worksheet for writing objectives.

Section 2: Games

Game 1: What are you doing game. Two students stand in front of the class. One starts pantomiming an action. The other student says "what are you doing?" The first student keeps pantomiming the action but says a different action. The second student must start pantomiming the action. The first student then asks, "What are you doing? " The second student keeps their pantomime going and says a completely different action, the first student must start pantomiming this new action and so on.

Game 2: Give a list of four activities for students to do such as preparing to take a trip. Have them perform four activities that demonstrate the action. Such as, get a suitcase, get your clothes, put them in the case, shut the case, leave the room.....

Game 3: Mirror. Have students partner up. One person leads and the other person follows. The students place their hands up to a mirror and begin movements one leading one following. Then try full body, one person leads in movement and the other follows. Then try scenes. Two people will do a simple scene, eat a sandwich or brush their teeth. Another two people are "in the mirror" and follow the first two people. The goal is to be synchronized where you do not know who is the lead and who is the reflection.

Section 3: Scene Work

Scene Work

With your scene partner do the following work and check it off when you are done.

- Talk about your moment before entering the scene
- Talk about what you want in the scene
- Talk about where you go after the scene
- Improvise your moments before entering.
- Improvise your scene
- Improvise your moments after exiting
- Rehearse your scene once with the script
- Rehearse your scene without your script

Section 4: Assessment

Each student group will perform their scene without words showing their scene only through actions and movements.

Know Your Objective

Acting is doing. A play is about action. The performer's duty is to find the action and through movement and dialogue reveal this action to the audience.

The best way for a performer to know their action is to know their beats of actions and find their objective for each beat. Knowing what your character wants gives you the action to create a life and authentic play. Create I want statements for your character I want_____. Then you do everything in your power to get that want met.

The actor needs to make the characters want very important. The stronger the need and the more powerful the desire to fill that need, the more compelling and committed the actor becomes. Audiences want to see action. Characters emerge when Actors play the action. Every part of script analysis should compel you to action. When you explore the wants of a character make the want and need strong, powerful and necessary. The wants should be playable and at the end of the scene you should know if you got your goal or not.

1. Strong Needs and Wants create what?
strong action

2. Why should you make a characters needs important and action centered?
to play it strong. Know if you got your goal met or not by end of scene.

When you choose an objective…..

- Have an immediate objective for this moment,
- Have an overall objective for this scene, and
- Have a super objective.

You know you choose a good objective if you…

- are compelled to action,
- Energized, and
- Really connecting to your scene partners.

Creating an I want Statement:

Transitive verbs describe an act such as hit. Transitive verbs are active. They need an object in order for the word to make sense. Active verbs need interaction. Active verbs direct energy to a target. Active verbs are what an actor is looking for when he or she describes his wants in a scene.

What are Transitive Verbs?
action words

Creating an I want statement
3 main parts. Person, Strong verb, to another person

1. I want to (remember you are the character
2. strong actable verb (that really gets you fired up!)
3. Object or person (theatre is relationship and connections. You are on the stage acting and interacting. Know you need to get what you want from and then go for it with 100% commitment and power.

Strong I want Statements:
I want to…. Convince ….(object/person)
I want to…. Prove ….(object/person)
I want to . . . Destroy ….(object/person)
I want to . . . Soothe ….(object/person)
I want to . . . pacify….(object/person)
I want to . . . Compel….(object/person)

Active verbs:
Avoid
Challenge
Clarify
Declare
Defend
Establish
Examine
Identify
Intervene
Maintain
Reduce
Terminate
Testify
Undermine

Performance Fundamentals Level 2

Lesson 10: Emotions

Objective: The students will demonstrate knowledge of emotions by discussing their scenes and the emotions of the characters.

Section 1 Intellectual Time:

Emotions Worksheet and review

Section 2

Game 1: "Remember When"
Have the students close their eyes and relax. Have them visualize a memory. Create one using all five senses. Have them go home and visit a dying relative, their first carnival ride, or their first date. Help them get fully into a memory so that they can recreate the emotion of that time.

Game 2: Have two students come in front of the class. Give them a scene scenario to perform. The catch is that they can only say a nursery rhyme to each other. The point is to get the emotions hear, not to worry about the lines.

Game 3: "Quadrant Game"
Divide the playing space into four sections. Give each section an emotion. Have two people get up and perform a scene. The couple will move at various times to the different quadrants incorporating the emotion belonging to that quadrant.

Section 3 Scene Work

Scene Work: Blocking Rehearsals.

Example: Have a group come to the front of the room. Have them perform their script and write down their movements, or blocking. Answer any questions before people break up into their groups.

Scene Work:

Check off the blocks when you have finished the work.

- o ☐ choose a prop and use to show your inner life
- o ☐ find a center of gravity for your character
- o   Decide on a mystery or secret for your character
- o ☐ Practice Your scene with The script.
- o ☐ Practice Your scene without the Script.

Section 4
Assessment: Have each group describe and improvise their scenes to the class paying special attention to the mood and feelings of the characters.

Materials: Lines from nursery games
Signs to make different emotions for quadrants.

EMOTIONS

Audiences do not come to see you show an emotion. They come to experience the emotion. The audiences want to see a person struggle inspite of their emotions to succeed at their goal. They want to feel the emotion you are fighting against. They want to see you fight for your goal and they want to celebrate when you win and grieve when you cry.

1. What do audiences come to the theatre to do?
Feel emotions

Performances are all about honesty. It does not matter what you do with your hands, or what emotion you are showing, nor does it matter if you can make yourself cry on stage. What does matter is honesty. Are you honest with your characterization. Are you honestly fighting for your goals. Are you honest in your intent to reach your objectives. If you are honestly fighting for your needs and wants to be met, the emotion will be there, and the audience will live within you.

2. _T_ T/F performances are about honesty.

When a director or script calls for a certain emotion, do not present the emotion. Take time to create memories and an emotional life for the character that will uphold the called for emotion. If the script says: (grimace before your line) You are going to create a history that would cause you to grimace. Then, during the performance trust that the inner life is there and will produce real emotions for that needed scene.

3. What do you do if you are told to produce a certain emotion?
Create a life experience to give a foundation for that emotion to naturally occur.

When you have an objective and know what you are fighting for and submerse yourself in the characters action, the right emotions will be there. Focus on doing not on showing,

4. What happens if you focus on the action?
Emotion naturally arises.

Acting Fundamentals Level 2

Performance Fundamentals Level 2

Lesson 11: Tactics. Get what you want.

Objective: Students will demonstrate the importance of getting what they want by performing the climax of their scene where they go for broke fighting to win.

Section 1: Intellectual

Student Work: What do I have to do to get it worksheet.

Lecture Notes: Review the Worksheet. Refer to the scene scoring worksheet for writing tactics and obstacles.

Section 2: Games

Game 1: The students will be instructed to partner up with someone on their team. One partner is given a fortune cookie. They open it and read the fortune. The other partner will give a response of over three words. The exchange goes on until each person has responded at least five times. If each accurately and effectively do five responses a point is earned for their team.

Game 2: Students will improvise a job interview scene. The students choose a strong motivation they need the job because…….. The job interviewer is distracted because of allergies, a head ache, a cute secretary .. . . . The first student has to overcome all obstacles and persuade or convince the job interviewer to hire them.

Game 3: Tongue Twisters. Read a tongue twister then ask a parent for the keys to the car but you can only say the tongue twister.

Game 4: Numbers. Two students do a scene together. They can only say the same four numbers. 1234 or 7658 something like that. One student must greet the other student by saying their numbers and then ask a question The scene can only be the four numbers you choose to say.

Section 3: Scene Work

Each student has a copy of the scene work in their unit packet.

Scene Work

With your scene partner do the following work and check it off when you are done.

- Go through your scene without breaking focus or character
- Perform your scene conscientious of stage and movement
- Break your script into beats of action.
- Write what you want beside each beat of action
- Perform your scene focused on motivation, stakes, and energy
- Go through your scene ready for performances.

Section 4: Assessment

Students will perform one minute of there scene. Choose the climax and make it powerful and important.

Tactics

When you know what you want, and it is worth fighting for. You have to invest 100% of your energy into getting that want. That is where tactics come in to play.

You want a specific thing from someone. You have an obstacle. Something stands in your way of getting that want. Each beat of action should have two to three tactics for fighting for that want. When you are on stage fighting for your want you use the tactic to try and get it. If the tactic does not work, you try another tactic. At the end of each beat of action, you should know if you won or lost.

1. What is a tactic?
The way you try to get what you want.

When you do beat rehearsals where you do each beat of action three times, experiement with different tactics to fight for your objective. How do your scene partners respond to you when you use different tactics? Does one tactic work better than another in a particular scene or beat of action?

Tactics...
If my objective is I want to SOOTHE so and so in order to get the keys to the car my first tactic might be
Convince (I am capable)
Prove I am responsible
And the third tactic might be to complement mom to get the keys.

So I want the keys. My goal is to soothe and calm my mother. I will convice, prove and complement. Try three different things to get the keys.

Obstacles
Drama happens because of conflict. Performers reveal inner conflict, relationship conflict or life conflicts on the stage. That is what ever plot, scene, and beat of action revolves around. You have to know what stands in your way of getting what you want. What are you fighting for? And, what are you fighting against. Make your obstacle as clear and powerful as possible and then do everything in your power to defeat this obstacle and get what you want.

2. What is an obstacle?
The person that stands in your way of getting what you want.

Performance Fundamentals Level 2
Lesson #12: Characterization

Objective: Students will demonstrate the character they will perform by crossing the stage and greeting their scene members in character.

Section 1: Intellectual

Students will work on Character Sketch and Scene Scansion. A unit delving into characterization is coming soon!

Section 2: Games

Game 1: Visualize yourself walking into a room. What can you smell? Is the room old or new? You notice a desk in the corner. Is it a small or large desk? Is the wood bright and polished or old and warn? You notice a letter poking out of a drawer. What sort of paper is it? Is it lined or stationary? Is it fresh or has it been there for a while. Take the letter out of the drawer. Open it up and read it. Wait a minute. You fold the letter up and place it back in the drawer. Notice the resistance of the drawer as you close it. You look around the room and walk out. Listen to your foot steps as you walk out of the room. Picture yourself walking up to the school and into this room. Now open your eyes and look around.

Game 2: Each student will be given a person such as a hair dresser, a banker, a grocery worker…. They will pantomime the person and the class will guess who the person is.

Game 3: Entrances: Give a student a place to walk into. They are a doctor who just received the test results going in to explain them to a patient… or a burglar who is entering a house. Have the students pantomime an entrance.

Game 4: Joining in. One student begins a scene pantomiming an activity. When another student figures it out, they come and join in. Continue adding three to four students. Example would be a rock band. One student starts with a guitar and so on…

Section 3: Scene Work
Each student has a copy of scene work activities in their unit book.

Scene Work

With your scene partner do the following work and check it off when you are done.

- o Read through the script moving on your set.

- o Place your script down and improvise through your scene.

- o Read through your script moving on your set.

- o Place your script down and improvise through your scene

- o Read through your script moving on the set

- o Place your script down and improvise through your scene.

On your own:

- o Create your character sketch.

Section 4: Assessment

Each student will cross the stage and greet each other in character.

Performance Fundamentals Level 2
Lesson 13: Performances

Step 1: Quiz

Step 2: Performances

Step 3: Evaluations

Every Unit is intense and action packed. A couple of nice quiet days in the library is a wonderful time to integrate and get ready for the next action packed unit.

Library Days
Student Assessment:

Student Name:_____ Date:_____

Parent/librarian/teacher supporter: _____

___1. Read a play.

___2. Found a scene/monologue and photo copied it.

___3. Got Thespian records up to date working towards honor medal at graduation.

___4. Got scene and character sketch scanned and saved working towards portfolio.

___5. Got resume and head shot up to date working towards high school portfolio.

Game Day

This is a nice way to find or cultivate talent for the School Comedy Club.

Play students favorite Games

Pattern a class period after the comedy club

Use a resource such as Comedy Sports International and use their game playing agendas.

Anita Jesse's The Playing is The Thing is a great resource for student games.

Evaluation

Name: Date:

Quality	Points Poss.	Points Recvd.	Comments
Set and Staging	20		
Movement and Prop	20		
Physicalization	10		
Effective Dialogue	10		
Relationship Established	10		
Memorized	20		
Stay in Character	10		

Evaluation

Name: Date:

Quality	Points Poss.	Points Recvd.	Comments
Set and Staging	20		
Movement and Prop	20		
Physicalization	10		
Effective Dialogue	10		
Relationship Established	10		
Memorized	20		
Stay in Character	10		

Testing in a Theatre Arts Environment

Many schools require a written mid-term and Final Exam turned in with an answer key. Having Quizzes builds to mid term and Final Exams.

The Quizzes and Tests are not meant to stress the students. They are more of a gesture of conformity and acceptance of the education environment.

Quizzes and Tests are good for emergencies if a person cannot come to exams, this applies to teachers, maternities and FMLA emergencies as well.

Questions for a theatre test need to be concrete. There are a lot of different answers that could make any answer write and can make a test very subjective.

The quizzes in the units are meant to help with retention, be concrete, and are usually scored in the worksheet section. If a class needs more motivation then the quiz scores are placed in performance category.

Acting Fundamentals Level 2
Quiz

Name: Date:

1. Why should a performer know who to relax?

2. What are the four parts of script analysis?
Read the script three times like a novel
Understand the structure and flow of the play.
Know your beats of action.
Daydreaming

3. What do you do after all the script analysis is done?

4. What must the actor concentrate on?

5. What must the character concentrate on?

6. What is the fourth wall?

7. Why should you spend time observing people and places?
_____

8. Why do you need to know the theme?
_____

9. Why should you know the events of the play?
_____

Check off the actor's work:
10. What are three things the actor needs to know when exploring the events of a play?
Where he or she is and feels about it
What you are having for lunch
what are the discoveries the character makes
where are the turning points that changes the flow of events.

11. Why do you use all five senses when you imagine?
_____

Check off the right answers
12. What are three things a performer uses their imagination to create?
Character
moment before
relationships
food menu
play structure

Check off the right answer
13. Why should you know the physical location, emotional memories, and relationships of the scene?
It is interesting
It affects a persons behavior and thoughts.
It is required for the grade

Acting Fundamentals Level 2

14. What are the two keys to using your imagination as specified in this unit?

15. ___ T/F listening is an active Skill.

16. ___ T/F listening is waiting for a cue

17. Strong Needs and Wants create what?

18. Why should you make a characters needs important and action centered?

19. What do audiences come to the theatre to do?

20. ___ T/F performances are about honesty.

21. What do you do if you are told to produce a certain emotion?

22. What happens if you focus on the action?

23. What is a tactic?

24. What is an obstacle? _____

Quiz
Answer Key

1. Why should a performer know who to relax?
Gives control over the body, the actors tool.

2. What are the four parts of script analysis?
Read the script three times like a novel
Understand the structure and flow of the play.
Know your beats of action.
Daydreaming

3. What do you do after all the script analysis is done?
Let it go and trust that it has created your creative foundation

4. What must the actor concentrate on?
Lines staging, props, movements

5. What must the character concentrate on?
The objectives and getting them met.

6. What is the fourth wall?
Pretending that there is a screen or wall between you and the audience….

7. Why should you spend time observing people and places?
Creates truthful knowledge to how people behave and respond for accurate presentations.

8. Why do you need to know the theme?
Theme is the purpose that unifies a cast and crew.

9. Why should you know the events of the play?
To know what your purpose is, to know what you are doing.

Check off the actor's work:
10. What are three things the actor needs to know when exploring the events of a play?
Where he or she is and feels about it
What you are having for lunch
what are the discoveries the character makes
where are the turning points that changes the flow of events.

11. Why do you use all five senses when you imagine?
To make memories real and strong.

Check off the right answers
12. What are three things a performer uses their imagination to create?
Character
moment before
relationships
food menu
play structure

Check off the right answer
13. Why should you know the physical location, emotional memories, and relationships of the scene?
It is interesting
It affects a persons behavior and thoughts.
It is required for the grade

14. What are the two keys to using your imagination as specified in this unit?
Awareness and trust.

15. _T_ T/F listening is an active Skill.

16. _F_ T/F listening is waiting for a cue

17. Strong Needs and Wants create what?
strong action

18. Why should you make a characters needs important and action centered?
to play it strong. Know if you got your goal met or not by end of scene.

Acting Fundamentals Level 2

19. What do audiences come to the theatre to do?
Feel emotions

20. _T_ T/F performances are about honesty.

21. What do you do if you are told to produce a certain emotion?
Create a life experience to give a foundation for that emotion to naturally occur.

22. What happens if you focus on the action?
Emotion naturally arises.

23. What is a tactic?
The way you try to get what you want.

24. What is an obstacle?
The person that stands in your way of getting what you want.

Scene Scoring

Beat #	I want…	From…	Tactic	obstacle

Write your beat number.

Write what you want.

Write who you want it from – action is reaction – relationships – even if you are alone on stage.

Tactic – what are you willing to do to get it – how>

Obstacle – what stands in your way of getting what you want.

Make your I want statements big. Go for broke in your fight for what you want. Win or Loose make it big, make it real, and fight for it till the bitter end.

Acting Fundamentals Level 2

Participation Points

Student	Lesson 1	Lesson 2	Lesson 3	Lesson 4	Lesson 5	Scene Partner

Participation Points

Student	Lesson 6	Lesson 7	Lesson 8	Lesson 9	Lesson 10

Participation Points and Overall Points

Student	Lesson 11	Lesson 12	Lesson 13	Teacher Comments

Classroom Management

A busy class stays on task. ¼ time intellectual work. ½ the time games and scene work. ¼ time assessment. This break down of time keeps a class moving in positive ways.

A graded scene every two weeks keeps a class busy and working hard towards a goal.

A theatre class must start silent and end silent. Creative classes can spin out of control if a teacher cannot constantly keep a structured foundation. Beginning and ending in a very structured way keeps the class aware of when to be silent and when to be loud….
Holding a class after the bell for speaking in these first few minutes or last few minutes is sufficient motivation for keeping it silent.

Obeying school standards and keeping high standards on the stage is important. The first student who swears or uses negative gestures should be held after the bell, given lunch d-hall and given a referral immediately. One person taking a huge active consequence fast keeps the other 24 from attempting that behavior.

Classroom Tracking

Date: Class:

Check indicates repeated student behavior

Student Name:

	Week	Week	Week	Week
1. Failure to follow instructions 2. Not doing Work 3. No Materials				
Overt Behavior: 1 Defiance/insubordination 2. Refusal to obey 3. Talking Back				
Subtle Behavior: 1. Non-verbal (body Language) 2. Gestures 3. Defiance				
Away from assigned position in room without permission.				
Disrespect student/ teacher / aid				
Secondary Behavior: 1. Posturing 2. Inciting 3. Contributing to others behavior				
Assault / Physical Behavior				
School Rules (clothes, electronics, food)				
Refusal To Take Responsibility				

Teacher Responses:
Verbal Warning:

Student / Teacher Conference:

Teacher Discipline:

Parent / Teacher Conference:

Acting Fundamentals Level 2

Theatre Arts Behavior Report

Student _____ Date _____

      Educational research has consistently shown that when a teacher spends excessive class time managing discipline problems, less teaching and student learning occur. In theatre classes, time is given to individual work which allows the teacher to work one on one with each group and every student. However, the personal training time is dependent upon the entire class being on task.

I regret to inform you that your son or daughter exhibited the following misbehavior during class which prevented a positive education environment:

Failure to follow instructions
Failure to bring appropriate materials
Excessive talk, noise, and/or sounds
Foul or disturbing language
Failure to be in the appropriate place with the correct partner.
Talking and/or not paying attention while the teacher is lecturing
Discourteous conduct towards other students
Refusal to participate
Misconduct during performances
Not taking responsibility for actions or behavior
Unit work not competed nor turned in.

Additional comments and explanations:

_____

_____

_____

Please sign this form and have your son or daughter bring this back to class.
Please call for a parent / teacher conference.

_____
Parent signature   Date

Thank you.

Acting Fundamentals Level 2

Made in the USA
Lexington, KY
06 August 2014